Shadows on Wood

poems by

Lacy Snapp

Finishing Line Press
Georgetown, Kentucky

Shadows on Wood

Copyright © 2021 by Lacy Snapp
ISBN 978-1-64662-696-0 First Edition
All rights reserved under International and Pan-American Copyright Conventions. No part of this book may be reproduced in any manner whatsoever without written permission from the publisher, except in the case of brief quotations embodied in critical articles and reviews.

ACKNOWLEDGMENTS

Previous appearances for poems: A few were published twice, the second being in an anthology.

"Red Oak;" "Heartpine" ~ *The Mockingbird*
Women of Appalachia Project's *Women Speak*, Volume Six
"Us Middle School Nymphs" ~ Women of Appalachia Project's *Women Speak*, Volume Six

I am eternally grateful for my parents, Debbie and Mike, for giving me life, supporting me as I discover myself, and passing down so many of these familial stories that have impacted my identity.

A special thanks goes to my father and grandfather, P.C. Snapp, for teaching me the craft of woodworking, which has changed the way I interact with world around me. Finally, I would like to thank my poetry mentors and M. Daniel McCrotty for ruthlessly encouraging my writing.

Publisher: Leah Huete de Maines
Editor: Christen Kincaid
Cover Art: Lacy Snapp
Author Photo: Michael Snapp
Cover Design: Elizabeth Maines McCleavy

Order online: www.finishinglinepress.com
also available on amazon.com

Author inquiries and mail orders:
Finishing Line Press
PO Box 1626
Georgetown, Kentucky 40324
USA

Table of Contents

Lore 1

Red Oak 2

Cedar 4

Heartpine 6

This Is the Stuff of Nightmares 8

Addendum 10

Daily Routine—Ars Poetica 12

Railway Reckoning 14

Echoes of a Mockingbird 16

Fragility. Transparency. Kitchen Light Fixture. 17

Liminal 18

Becoming a Ghost 19

Red Thong at the North Chickamauga Blue Hole 20

A Sharper God 21

Tell Me 22

Us Middle School Nymphs 24

Sylvia and the Sycamores 26

Bloody Marys in the Water 28

Destruction. Creation. A Black Hole. 30

Wormy Chestnut 31

Lore

Green and blue grain, purple that borderlines on black
stretches out beneath my hands as I pull lumber
out of the back of my dad's truck. *It's called rainbow
poplar*, he says in a voice that to me feels ancient
and all-knowing, like he's letting me in on a secret
available only to a select few. *Next to a mountain stream
that tree grew, pulling, pulling in nutrients from
a source deep within the earth.* As I gaze deep within
its rings, I can see myself. A Gemini-moon mix of different
personalities. I, too, have pulled from the world
around me. Purple patches from traveling, experiences
that forever changed a young Johnson City girl. Blue
waves of insecurities forged once the universe became
bigger—black streaks of bad habits picked up from people
who I now realize were just as lost as me. Greenness
that tries to hold on to the person I once was. As we stack
the wood inside the shop, I find each board is drastically
different—a cosmic affirmation that I will also continue
to change, evolve as I pull, pull from what's around me.
To this day, I don't know if my dad's legend is even true,
and I haven't the heart to find out, research if he is wrong.
I prefer to be the barefoot young woman, ankle deep
in the creek, absorbing what's around me, wondering
what future story a two-inch slice of my soul will tell.

Red Oak

I.
RIP my childhood red oak.

When you were planted by my father,
you were only the height of a toddler,
but grew to be three stories tall
and would brush your tree-tips across
my bedroom window at midnight,
relentlessly throughout summer storms.

You were the first tree I ever climbed.
It was uncomfortable—I'd hug tight
to your trunk when I needed a rest,
bark would poke through my shirt
into my soft, elementary belly. I felt
ants scurry beneath fingertips but
I was too scared of falling to ungrip.

Fresh-faced stump, you now stare up
at me. In shock. Outraged. Wounded.
Years of shade and afternoon games
dropping sap and acorns on my car
were cut away in a few hours—
a deception that shook every house
on the street, rippled out from the eye
of your rings, confined now to seventeen.

II.
RIP backroad red barn.

You offered wanderers protection as they
braced against the elements in the middle
of a cow field. Unconcerned with
the modern—electricity, fashion—your red
paint flaked proudly until your sagging roof

and old age were no longer charming,
but dangerous. You fought my father with
each rusted nail as he tore you down.

I spread out your seventeen foot limbs,
stick stack sort them, make sure they stay
flat, are prepared to be cut and sanded,
formed into a table or clock, something less
mysterious than an untouched barn at a dirt
road's end. Your worth is now measured by
feet. Inches. How well you can be divided.

I flip your scarlet face away and watch as
silverfish scurry from my fingertips. Hating
the sunlight, but unafraid, when the wood's
movement disturbs them, a new home is
easily found. Soft. Grey. Fluid. Sheltered in
the solid bones of a red oak twice displaced.

Cedar

The last lumber haul of a man's life. His grandson in the passenger
seat of his brand new, 1959 sky blue Chevy Apache. Dirt roads
just to get there. Pappy starts whittling around the fire
with distant cousins of his mother, Mexico Ray, in North Carolina
backwoods. Smoking pipes. Chewing toothpicks. Speaking of
weather and other nothings, no business until they have to.
They load whatever cedar the truck can carry. Back home,
he uses a hand saw, hand sander, hand planer until his arms
are past sore. His grandson collects the shavings off the floor,
stores them in a blue Mason jar above his bed.

Pappy lines the new house's closets with that wood because it guards
against moths. That, and it's all he has. He makes chests, armoires.
Any vessel that will keep clothes fresh as they're surrounded
by live edge. As he sits in his yellow arm chair, wearing his
Sunday suit, Granny starts supper in the kitchen—swats eager
fingers looking to swipe morsels off the stove. She gives nothing
away, scraps or her thoughts, just stirs, snaps homegrown
green beans—enlists idle children to do the same.

A room away, he baits the youngest grandchildren with butterscotch
candy, tries to disguise the strong undertones of his Horehound
liquorish breath. Gets them to feel safe, then pinches their sides
until they scream and fight his sunburnt arms and stone grip.
Late afternoon, hallway closet jacket on, he walks through
the backyard garden to tend to the grapevine and pick ripe apples
for the cellar, the giant pear tree hums with a nearby passing train.

In view of the kitchen window, he tucks his hand into his coat pocket,
finds a clump hair—red as a newly exposed, fresh cut cedar log. *Lavada,
what did you do?* Their eyes meet somewhere above the garden's middle
as he heeds the warning from his wife: *Don't wander
over the mountain again to her,* the girl back in Shelton Laurel—
not even the cedar closet can protect their secret now. The locks fall
into the grass atop cherries split by the recent rain. He lights his pipe

tobacco, smoke clouds his face then rambles away with the evening breeze. The two gazes become fixed across wire-rimmed spectacles, pupils now unwavering as tree knots set in bark.

Heartpine

Juanita. Juanita.
We repeat words to ingrain them into memory.
Sometimes, the more we say a word, the stranger it feels
on the tongue. Foreign. Like we don't actually know what it means
at all. Juanita.
Great-grandmother. I knew her as a child. Well, parts of her. I knew
how she would sweeten her coffee with ice-cream. I knew her jewelry
stand by heart—I'd get on tiptoes to peer into every drawer, marvel
at the broaches, the rings, try with little fingers to clip
Sarah Coventry earrings onto little earlobes. I knew
her everyday necklace, pearls even and
tight like the grain of heart pine.
Heartpine.
When the tree's seed germinates,
for ten years it will only be the height of a blade
of grass. For ten years, its energy is spent strengthening
its root system—most of its universe lies beneath the surface.
When it's finally ready, it will grow an inch wider every thirty years.
After her death, I found black and white photographs of a woman
in a pencil skirt and pinned on hat, peeking out from behind a tree,
laughing, whiskey bottle in hand—I learned she slept with
a pearl handle Bauer .25 under her pillow and had five
husbands, some passed of mysterious
circumstances. She voyaged
from Shelton, NC, on a covered wagon with
her many brothers and sisters, dressed in matching
potato sacks, and looking back on the poorness of what was,
wasn't mournful, just wanted more. A pair of shoes for every blouse,
tools of her own, accessories, she'd write her name on anything
in Sharpie to claim it as it came through the door. Every pan
in the kitchen. Even the back wall of her father's cedar armoire.
One Sunday, after her second stroke, Dad loaded us up in the van
to pay her a visit. Measuring tape in his hand, she stood on her tiptoes,
eager for my dad to calculate her height, her width—he told her
that was cheating, she needed to keep her feet flat.

It took us a few months to build her coffin
in the basement.
I was only ten, friends would come over
for sleepovers and be scared of what was in the works beneath
the house's surface. In the end, when her growth rings were getting
closer and closer together, she'd ask dad how it was coming along
and he'd tell her, to hang on a bit longer,
he wasn't done yet. In a plot with a view at Happy Valley
Memorial Park, she is closer to being reunited
with the earth than those encased
in bronze or copper. She sleeps in a bed all her own,
made of reclaimed heartpine.
Heartpine for Juanita.

This Is the Stuff of Nightmares

I.
Knowing I need a shower—age eight,
I'd lock the bathroom door and let the water
run and run while I'd stand there, fully clothed.
Sometimes, I'd turn the water back off. Wait
for a while, let the steam seep beneath the door frame
until my face would appear in the mirror. Blink
a few times. Turn the faucet on again—knowing
I can't stall forever. Undress, go to step in, retract.
Take socks off. Make sure the curtain is sealed tight,
and safe. Head leaned back, I'd feel like someone
was standing right behind me. Spin around,
no one's there—just a child's overactive imagination.
Shampoo. I need to rinse, and try to without
closing my eyes. Impossible. But I'd rather let them burn
than feel so small and naked in the darkness
of my own mind—a place where creatures
lurk and wait for those simple moments
when I feel safe, new, clean from soap.

II.
Knowing funerals only from my father's side—age ten,
I'd dread getting dressed up to go see Great Uncle Junior
in his wheelchair beneath the stained-glass window
pop his glass eye out for the children
when our parents turned their backs.
Unknown people, distant cousins, die all the time
when you're young. Sit through countless versions
of "Amazing Grace." Try to stay awake,
maybe conjure a tear to not feel so out of place
among so many strangers dressed in black.
My uncle died when I was old enough to know the drill,
but this loss was different. Drunk driving accident—
when I was older my dad told me his no-seatbelt pickup truck
folded like an accordion when it collided with the overpass'
support beam. For that funeral, I opted out.

Offered to watch my little, first cousins—age three and six.
We played in the basement of his Knoxville home,
down the hall from his old room. Rolled out
his black sleeping bag. I crawled in, burrowed as deep
as I could. It smelled like feet, but it was warm,
padded, familiar. I waited for my older sister to return—
took one look at her face. Resented the day
there'd be no more cushioned caves to hide away in.

Addendum

October, you are the month of heat decaying
into greyness, accented by orange and yellow leaves
that descend slowly, like how human hair continues
to grow even after we are dead and buried
in our Sunday's best, six feet under, twelve feet
if we want a lover to slide in on top of us, touch eternally,
coffin to coffin. You are the painted skeleton faces
of Día de los Muertos, the clown masked man
at the end of my street, standing under the flickering
lamplight on All Hallows' Eve. You are the black cat
that crosses over my front porch—and that same familiar
that circles back in a Déjà Vu flashes two days later.
You are the trick-or-treat candy in a box I hoarded

under my bed as a child that has lain in wait, you
are that hand waiting to reach out and grab my ankles
from under the bed skirt when I'd get up to use the bathroom
in the middle of the night. You are the reason
why when I'd return, I'd leap from two feet away
to clear your reach. You are why I slept with the lamp light
on. Dad would complain about conserving energy,
I was more worried about saving my soul. You
are Beetlejuice's face waiting to pop up when I lift
the toilet seat lid, you are Harvey, the six foot,
three and a half inch tall rabbit standing on the other side
of the shower curtain, listening as I sing to myself.
You are why I'd run up the stairs from the dark basement

as a girl, afraid of demons nipping at my heels.
You still follow me. As I walk to my car after class
in an inexplicable fog, taunting me with acorns, back
to back surrounding sounds, shadows watching from behind
parked cars as I shiver from a chill that rolled in overnight.
On the drive home, I swear, carved face pumpkins follow
me with their gazes, their flickering candle eyes, their

wavering candle grins. One watches me from across
the street when I let the dog out, refuses to break eye contact.
I can still feel him watching as I try to fall asleep with
my childhood fears pressing down on me, bedside lamp
still on. October, you are a month of cold fingertips,
suppressions returned like someone back from the dead.

Daily Routine—An Ars Poetica

During the summers, I start pulling forgotten lumber
  from storage units every morning by eight a.m.
    The current stack—a mound of beech bowed from years
      of neglect. *It's shit wood anyways,* my dad says,
        splinters and cracks no matter how carefully it's handled.
Twelve feet above my head, I try to figure how
  I will manage to get it down—climb on the lower rows,
    pray they hold my weight, where random boards protrude
      like harpoons lost in Moby Dick's side.

While I ascend, simple phrases catch in my ears
  as spider webs do in my hair and branch out—spread,
    link together as I take little pieces from radio commercials
      or mainstream song lyrics that I wish I didn't know
        the words to. The first half
of the workday is a time for repeating: Step up. Balance.
  Pull the highest board out. Let it tip to the ground.
    Step off. Pick up. Carry to its new home. Double check
      that its aligned. Return to the stack—As my body shifts

into automation, my mind tests its ability to withstand
  the pressure of memory. A poem begins as the morning dew
    evaporates, starts with an image gathered
      unexpectedly: the perfectly preserved mouse carcass
        in a gap between two rows. Silverfish slipping
into their own reclaimed utopias. Carpenter bees flirting
  with overhead beams—while they tunnel, sawdust falls,
    sticking to the cobwebs I already wear, pairing together
      borrowed lyrics with beings that merely needed a voice.

Repeat until lunchtime, stomach growling and stanza
  about to burst from my mouth, I scavenge for a discarded
    block in the scrap box, settle for a two-by-four wedge.
      The poem pours out as my sandwich goes in, taking time between
        each bite to tap the cadence on my work bench stool.

For all the hours past noon, the stacking-lumber-process resumes
while my brain takes time to decompress. Pencil and cubed poem
in my pocket, I wait for the final words to find me—
unmistakable as a newly forged splinter beneath the skin.

Railway Reckoning

I.
Train conductor, step grandfather. He taught me to color, told me
the expected, to stay between the lines. The unexpected, to keep
my strokes traveling in the same direction, otherwise things seem
messy: arrangement reflects the mind's chaos. He passed away
in his sleep. No one mourned him like Meme did, or mourned him
at all. A third husband from Illinois, she couldn't find anyone
who wanted any of his ashes, no one except seven-year-old me.
Sentimental child, I was given a small cedar box packed with dust,
plus a few little bones, if I was lucky, a gold filling. As an adult,
I still keep this portion of a man I barely knew next to my bed,
whose soul was taken at daybreak as the train across from
Southwest Avenue swept through town.

II.
I fell out of love in a half-glass house tucked next to the end
of a train yard. An experiment of Chattanooga engineering students,
they ran out of money, and had to make do with recycled materials
to finish one side using just windows and some sealed sliding glass
doors beneath the staircase. The neighbors could watch the dishes
pile up from the street, dust collect in the corners. They knew when
we were awake, when asleep. They watched pothos vines grow
towards the wall of windows and tangle together, choking themselves
to get closest to the sun. Stagnant trains let out eerie moans throughout
the night. I never saw them coming, or going, always just resting
there in the fog, illuminated momentarily, every so often,
by blinking tower lights.

III.
Barefoot in the grass, I notice the blades fold in any direction
they want. My dog waits for me to throw the ball. Eager eyes,
obedient. The first day we met after being shipped from a breeder
in Texas, she was too terrified to get out of the kennel at the airport,
remained frozen from loud jet engines, the outbursts of an angry god.
It took time to trust me. Like me, she would jump at every little noise,

cower from books, cards, garbage trucks, folding clothes, table saws, the garden hose. Two years later, a train horn tries to shake the ground beneath our confident standoff. Neither of us move, hide beneath a bush, a shelter of incomplete protection. I wind up and release the ball. She is a force unstoppable. Carefree strides racing a steel steed in Founders Park, fearless, train screams fill her open mouth.

Echoes of a Mockingbird

The screen door leans, propped open by a stick
at the house across the empty lot.
Grass overgrown, never mowed,
the crape myrtle at the yard's edge
towers above but droops its pink
velour limbs on the roof—
In the two months I've lived next door,
I've never seen who lives there.
I watch the window's sheets for curtains
shift like someone's standing just behind them
observing as I lazily swing in my backyard.
The eight year old inside me
suspects it's Boo Radley as an elderly,
hunched over and alone without
a Scout for friendship. The cloth
on his back porch's chair is faded,
ripped, sagging, sad and low like it remembers
once being sat in, remembers early mornings
or late summer nights when it knew
the sensation of feeling whole, needed.
Then, the foundation's brick wasn't crumbling,
the electricity wasn't turned off,
the day's only worry was too many
mosquitos circling, or counting down until
the creeping heat from sun rays would stretch
across the porch, bringing with them
warmth a now-nocturnal man could not bear.

Fragility. Transparency. Kitchen Light Fixture.

I long to be dried flowers pressed between two pieces of glass.
I'd dwell in a glass house, exposed for everyone to see the bends
of my stems, the petals surrounding my head. My lopsided left fern leg.
My companion, a stink bug, now dead, and forever attached to my
right side. Without the clear security of my panes, I'd be nothing.
Just flora dust scattered by the wind, never again complete. I'd be
like all my former field companions, who bloomed, died,
and were returned to earth in their natural time.

Liminal

I tumble between who was and who is
like seed pods, descending.

Beneath the sturdy maple tree, my car
faithfully collects

the discards of the storm. When morning comes,
I take the back road to town

watching those gold helicopters fly
in the rearview mirror.

They don't apologize or say goodbye,
or look back, as I do.

They just move on to a new divot of
the sidewalk. To mingle with

trash escaped from bins, all newfound beings
who, too, have forgotten

places of birth, the branch from which they fell,
the garbage bag torn open

by the neighborhood's homeless dog. He wanders
endlessly, as I do.

Becoming a Ghost

Ghosts sit around my dining room table without place
settings. They follow neighborhood children to the bus
stop. Pass me the shampoo in the shower. Join me for
my morning stretches, downward-facing dog, ghost garbs
fall, cover their heads, reveal transparency. Two bicker
in the backseat on my drive to work, to the grocery store.
One doodles in the freezer aisle, gets distracted fogging glass
with his breath, drawing smiley faces with his silky ghost
fingers. A shopper reaches through him to get a frozen
pizza, my ghost glares, refuses to dissipate. Lady ghost
sits beside me in bed, complains about my tableside lamp,
it keeps her up. I click it off, lay silent in the blackness, replay
those moments that have long passed, moments I didn't speak
loud enough. My ghosts and I wander in Willow Springs Park.
I lead the V of this flock of geese, their linen white limbs billow
in the wind, scraps left behind like feathers on the grass.
They squawk at passersby, people who don't look at me—
chase these strangers to their cars, nipping at their heels.
One ghost sheds her veil, puts it in the tub to soak overnight.
When she isn't looking, I slip beneath the water, try it on, relish
in the unseen, love how it feels to officially have no face or name.

Red Thong at the North Chickamauga Blue Hole

because I wasn't prepared for swimming, I let the guys
climb up the embankment before me to the jump ledge.
Of course that didn't stop the strangers across the water
from getting a view, but at eighteen, I knew I'd never see
these Soddy Daisy locals again. From this new height,
the sun had already begun to dip behind the closest
ridgeline. A quick hike before dinner turned into the four
of us half naked, patiently waiting to expedite the cold,
wet walk back to the car. I hate going first, or second—
really just jumping at all. Freefalls make me nervous.
I look at the dark blue water and think: Aquarius,
a water sign, I'm supposed to want this, right? Sunlight
withdraws from the creek below, broken-beer-bottle glass
barely glistening between river rocks. Everyone else has jumped,
my friends and Soddy Daisy onlookers still wait for me to get the nerve.
I should want this. I should want this.

Months later, I sign waivers in the waiting room at Standard Ink
Tattoo, a block away from the Tennessee River. During my first
visit to Chattanooga before college, a woman jumped from
the Walnut Street Bridge just hours before our tour led us
to the shore's Riverwalk, and we watched search boats hoping
for a recovery. Now, only minutes away from getting my first tattoo,
a spontaneous rebellion with my roommate, the only symbol
I can think to choose are Aquarius waves: *make them blue,*
    the color of water.
Googling around for a design, I find what's been missing—
    no longer a misinformed air sign.

A Sharper God

I watch once green leaves yellow from direct sunlight.
The African violet sitting in the window sill sends me signs
it should be moved—shifted to the shelf across the room.
I wish it could be that simple, a small decision to pick it up
and set it down in partial shade. But six months ago, I impulsively
dropped two propagations into a clay pot together, resolved
to let them grow a little, relocate them if they lived through
the end of the month. But once settled, they slipped my mind.
I moved my focus to tending to the pothos, making new
clippings of the San Pedro, rotating the anthurium to see
if I could correct the uneven slant of the growing leaves.

Unnoticed, the cow horn cactus stalk and African violet
intertwined roots. One thriving from the light, and the other
singeing as a result. And yet, purple flowers still bloomed,
unfolded in harmony as fresh spikes emerged from its neighbor's
peak. As I decided they needed to separate, be rehomed
into conditions that would suite them best, they vowed
they wouldn't comply—star-crossed lovers who do not care
biology says they should not mix. So I pick the yellowed leaves
every week to leave room for fresh ones to grow, just to soon die.
I marvel as violet flowers give themselves as offerings again
and again to their constant sun-dial, their higher, sharper god.

Tell Me

Tell me, how can you regrow affection?

Can you just cut away at a relationship's dead limbs,
the ones that stopped us from communicating,
stopped us from looking one another in the eyes anymore?
They've held me back from apologizing
when I should—carrying my weight of the blame.

Tell me, how can you regrow affection?

Should we open ourselves up, slice at 45 degree angles
just beneath these pothos leaves, submerge into
Mason jars filled with water. Wait for roots to form—
as shy as the first time I really looked at you,
took your sight in from across the table. Unfurled myself
as a fresh sprout, waxy and new in the afternoon light.

Tell me, how can you regrow affection?

Waiting for those roots to emerge, changing the water,
two weeks with no result, I start to forget that
it's possible. I look for new sections to cut away at,
start over. Question if it wants to regrow at all.
Laser focused on all the leaves that have fallen, brown
and flaking on the floor, I ignore the newness on the ends,
the single drop of water that beads up like a blessing

from another world, tell me, can affection regrow?

Abundant as this pothos over the years
that went from a vine the size of my hand to one
with five strands that envelop the sunroom—I fold you
and me back together. As water roots venture out
from that blue glass jar with confidence like the first time
I let you kiss me—I begin to fill soil with intentions

that want to burrow deep, hold on for the long haul.
I'll tell you now, we can prune a little and direct our growth,
never make promises we can't keep, but vow to do better—
in small ways, daily, both when the vine ascends
by the window and when it dips back down from its own weight.
Let's mist one another in the hottest part of the day and not be afraid
of trimming back what doesn't do us any good.

Us Middle School Nymphs

Brood X cicadas bow down their brown bodies
to tree branches, camouflage behind emerald leaves
for privacy as they lay their eggs. Weeks later

new born nymphs drop down to the ground,
burrow beneath fresh earth to feast on tree roots' nectar
for the next seventeen years. The last time

they did this was in 2004—as eleven year old me
hid amidst swarms of prepubescent girls
in the new middle school hallway, tried to disappear

into acrylic murals painted onto walls of cinderblock:
scenes of Tennessee—the state flag, state flower,
state tree. I teetered on letting myself be seen,

only sometimes illuminating as the firefly does—
or would I call myself a lightning bug? Meanwhile,
boyish raccoon broods wrestled around every

corner. Mockingbirds whispered at the top of the stair.
*These insects appear in these fantastic numbers every
seventeenth year,* the Swedish naturalist Peter Kalm

noted in 1749 while visiting America. In prior years,
the woods brimmed with a different degree of dusk-silence—
only a lonely cicada or two. Some of Brood X emerged

prematurely in 2017, with whispers of the end of days
close behind. Scientists wondered why the group would divide,
why some were ready to surface years early, climb

the closest vertical object to shed outer layers and expand wings.
The answer can't be narrowed down to a scientific formula.
Ascending to middle school doesn't mean an immediate

shift for all—I watched as girls my age stuffed push-up bras
and began straightening their hair, decorating their faces
all in time for the morning announcements—shedding soft layers

as the tulip poplar in autumn: golden cardigans draped
over chair backs—daring the teacher to demand them
to re-dress: cover camisole tank top straps, thin and brown

as the topmost branches of the tree's canopy.
Some of us chose to stay beneath the ground for longer.
Waiting to emerge shyly as the Iris, purple petals

unfolding in early May. Or until a warm June's evening
to finally expand hard wing casings, the ones
simultaneously guarding me and holding me back.

I now unveil at twilight: a firefly—I decided.
Not beneath fluorescent bulbs or within walls of stone.
An intricate being made of fire and flight.

Sylvia and the Sycamores

Student papers and assignment rubrics stack
around me like adolescent sycamores trees
longing to grow faster. After hours of grading
I feel nothing but their weight, so I slowly slip
myself beneath them in my bed, afraid of disturbing
their shape. Like the silent forest creek, I follow
the only path available to me. Legs curve
to the left, then slightly right. Feet burrow under
American Lit II papers that threaten to spill
onto the floor. I cover up with the top sheet
and Freshman project proposals, close my eyes,
repeating: I can't fall asleep. There's too much
to do, too many students waiting for feedback,
draining this wooded water source so they
can quantify their height, their grade, their fate.
I check the time. T-minus eight hours until
my first class. Of exclaiming, *Who's ready
to discuss some American Literature*, barely after
8 AM. Of getting only tired eyes in return.
I know I'm not ready. And even though
I'm excited to teach Confessional Poetry,
I'll confess just for you, in this poem, I want
to call it off. Take a mental health day
on the day we're meant to talk about Plath.
About Sexton. Because although *I, a smiling woman
am not yet thirty,* I am drowning under waves
of Times New Roman and one inch margins.
Of saying, put a period here. Not there.
The end of the semester is made up
of *sticking myself together with glue,*
swallowing my exhaustion for the sake of
the performance. Of scribbling on the board
so they have something to write down.

Going line by line and asking *what can we
take away from this?* Tomorrow, for once,
I want to call it off. For the personal wellness
days that academia doesn't talk about enough.
So I do. Send out the email because I'm sure
they need it, too. But no weight is lifted.
Now, it is just accompanied by guilt that sits
like a barred owl on the branch of the closest
sycamore stack. His gaze is unwavering as
my eyes are all that peek out from the top sheet,
my form unrecognizable beneath layers of white.

Bloody Marys in the Water

Heat lightning, frogs croak
next to our gray beach house—
a structure soon to be forgotten,
but still resilient: a defiant middle finger
among the commercialized pastels.

Offshore, an oil rig spews fire.
We cut the engine. Bait our hooks
with scraps of smaller fish. It's red
snapper season—our family's patriarchs
go out from dawn until every drop

of sunlight fades. They bring us kids
along so their haul can be at max
capacity. I catch my two quickly, but
my brother throws back fish after fish,
mangling some in the process. He wants

the glory of the day's best specimen,
so he keeps his finger patiently pressed
to the line, waiting for movement,
Bud Light in his opposite hand. I watch
his rejects float next to the boat, fish

now foreign on top of water. Their blood
attracts the monster snappers from
the deep, dolphins swim up out of curiosity,
and hunger—I know they have to feel
the vibrations of their cousins' final struggles

inside the cooler by my feet. The matriarchs
drink bloody marys on the beach. Neglect
their sunscreen, save it for the youngest
grandchildren, and me. Chairs angled
toward the sun, books are meant for

light reading and shading our eyes.
I nap on a lumpy bed of sand,
wade out to wash off and watch
as millions of silver shiners part
around me. Waves fold over

my shoulders. Across the beach
a man and his son cast from
the shoreline, but they don't know
what they're doing—they catch
a too-small fish and rather than

cut the line, they drag the rod from
side to side, hoping the animal
will unhook itself. Instead, the fish
remains defiant, glaring with black
opal eyes, taking in his first and only looks

at blue air. Speechlessly prays for
the decency of either a clean kill
or a clean release—all to the tune of
an ice-cream truck jingle on repeat,
toddlers shrieking on the beach.

Destruction. Creation. A Black Hole.

Four-year old Rosie doodles in the storm door's
condensation, switching between her two index fingers.
Her left is reserved for straight lines, creating
known shapes, those indisputable facts:
she has a mother, and a dog. They live in
a two-story house with four Bradford Pear trees
along the street. The right sketches less tangible
things: her newly acquired imaginary
best friend, a six foot, eight-inch-tall rabbit
with big loops for his ears, stars for the points
of his bow tie. She gives the sun a face, both
male and female, bushy eyebrows,
a sharp chin, and rays that wrap around
the head like a diadem. On the outermost
edge, she draws a donut shape, alternating
between her two tools. *It's the black hole,*
she says in a dream-like state as her reflection
bounces back at her, her iris perfectly framed
by the final depiction. *I can see my whole life
from here.* Before now, the image
was unknown—a myth kept hidden
in the back of the mind. But on the cusp
of 2020, legends reveal themselves
as the capacity to create rests in the tips
of a small child's fingers,
and the ability to destroy: a quick and
unapologetic wipe from the palm of her hand.

Wormy Chestnut

The wormy chestnut clock chimes every fifteen minutes, without fail.
Sitting atop the living room mantel, since childhood it has alerted me
of passing time. Of the school bus at the end of the cul-de-sac
that's about to leave me—shoes in hand I'd have to sprint through
the backyard, flailing my arms, praying for the driver's mercy and that
my now wet socks weren't all for nothing. Tiptoeing to the bathroom
past midnight, I'd wait for the chimes to step on the creaky parts
of the hardwood flooring next to my parents' room. My father,
a carpenter, couldn't help himself from making a second clock
that greets visitors at the front door, but he never managed to sync
them up—fifth grade friends would come over for sleepovers
and not understand how I could stand the two trying to one up
each other every hour, wanting to prove their opinion of the exact
minute was the truest north.

In Piney Flats, the Snapp log cabin homestead stands with shutters
wide open, watching the times change and leave the past behind.
Silent and abandoned, cows graze next to the front porch, accustomed
to this unorthodox normalcy. In the den, the walls are made of thin
slats of wood, covered again and again with layers of paint
and wallpaper—teal, navy, or pink, a paisley or floral print. We peel
back those personality changes with the blades of our pocketknives,
curious of who is hiding beneath. Finally, a chestnut face peeks
through, but the grain is uncorrupted by holes, proving its pre-1900
age. After the blight infestation, beetles bore into the bark
for nutrients, leaving a network of pores in their wake. But the artifact
we uncover is blemish free, and seems to know just how unique it is—
lying in wait, storing its secret between undisturbed lines of brown
grain. Now, still-growing American Chestnut trees are almost
impossible to find, and their ancestors are hidden away by layers
of paint in backwoods homesteads.

As a preteen, I learned that I'm not a Snapp by blood. My father
was adopted, yet I still feel sentimental towards a heritage that
isn't really my own. For my first house as an adult, he built me

my own arched-top mantel clock, but since I haven't a fireplace
to put it on, it perches on a hemlock table outside my bedroom door.
My partner isn't used to the noise, so every fifteen minutes
he is startled, then annoyed. I have not heard the sound consistently
in years—every chime makes me think of my father, then regret
that I don't see him enough. Mostly, every quarter hour I am reminded
that so many seconds have silently tiptoed away. My partner feels
their echo throughout each room, but my ears are attuned to the sound
resonating and growing louder somewhere deep within its origin—
and me—it burrows extensively through those wormy chestnut holes
into the hidden dimension it holds at its center, one removed from both
time and space, in which ancestors by marriage wait to meet me, a place
in which I can make up for all that's slipped away.

Lacy Snapp possesses the dual spirit of both a poet and a carpenter. Born and raised in Johnson City, TN, she graduated with her BA in Creative Writing from University of Tennessee at Chattanooga and her MA in English from East Tennessee State University. She now teaches American Literature and Composition in the Department of Literature and Language at ETSU. In between her two degrees, she worked as carpenter with her father in her hometown, learning a family trade that has been passed down for generations. Lacy's father, Mike Snapp, took down 74 barns over a two year period in the greater East Tennessee area, saving that wood from being burned or destroyed due to urban sprawl. She started her own woodworking business in 2016, Luna's Woodcraft, which makes custom creations and vends craft events. Her art specializes in using this reclaimed barnwood, giving these ancient trees a new life, though she also utilizes other species from the area. That firsthand experience with different woodgrains inspired Lacy to associate those characteristics to qualities and memories of various family members, which was the seed for this chapbook. Locally, she is a board member for the Johnson City Poets Collective which facilitates spoken word events for the community. She is currently an MFA in Writing candidate at Vermont College of Fine Arts. Her life is full thanks to her partner, Raleigh, her beloved border collie, Ruby.

www.ingramcontent.com/pod-product-compliance
Lightning Source LLC
LaVergne TN
LVHW041508070426
835507LV00012B/1413